Guide to Street

Christie Moore

authorHOUSE®

AuthorHouse™ UK Ltd.
500 Avebury Boulevard
Central Milton Keynes, MK9 2BE
www.authorhouse.co.uk
Phone: 08001974150

Published by AuthorHouse 1/16/2012

ISBN: 978-1-4678-8327-6 (sc)
ISBN: 978-1-4678-8328-3 (e)

Christie Moore's Guide to street

Based on observations around Britain

Written and illustrated by Christie Moore   ©2011

Guide to Street

Many young people live on the streets of Britain either permanently or when the parents have thrown them out of the house. They gather in large groups for safety and spend time just hanging around, or if they have money, pay to go into somewhere and just hang around. Many of these people have worthless lives with little or no ambition, which is not to say they never have money. They just hang around on streets with their own language and with the freedom to do (literally) what they like.

They have their own identity and are often referred to as chavs, not all street people are chavs, and not all chavs are street people, but there is a huge overlap between the two. No one really knows where the word chav came from but the Romani word for child is chavi, however the favourite definition is that it stands for Council House And Violent, a more appropriate term. There are many other names for them such as hoodies or ASBO generation, but chav is the most well known and the term used when someone to describe the yob in the most derogatory way possible. Sometimes female chavs are known as chavettes.

Chavs do not belong to a particular class as there can be posh chavs, although educated and chav together in the same phrase is a contradiction. It's the way they behave that defines them as a chav, and whatever their class background, chavs will always be 'oiks of the first order'.

Christie Moore's Guide to Street

Language

They have their own language, or rather lack of it. They just don't use words unless they are recognised street terms. Quite often, they don't mean anything but as long as they are uttered, then the chav will be accepted into chav society. They often talk to each other but have no idea what each other are saying.

Many words are repeated, as chav vocabulary is limited. I am, you are and he/she is are all indistinguishable to a chav and they refer to I is, you is and he/she is. Grammar is an alien concept to them. These words they use are key words that are readily accepted by other chavs as being street cred and will be a kind of password to the gang. Even if the word is used in the wrong meaning it doesn't matter, it's a recognisable word.

To get an idea of the way they speak, here is a quote from chavworld.co.uk:

"peeps say dat chavs r scum ye! wel u peeps dat say dat blatently ent look in da ******* mira at ur life recently jus cuz we av fights an **** dun make us bad boyz an galz ye! so nxt time u go round sayin **** bout us u cn rememba dat we got beta lives dan u wil eva av !!!"

(The spellchecker went crazy for this passage)

Education

Don't swear they have none! Chavs like to be stupid; any sign of a maths equation or Shakespeare quote will result in a duffing, as education is uncool. However, chavs do show signs of intelligence every now and then, like when demobilising an alarm in order to steal a car, or complex workings out to claim what they are owed by the state.

Chavs can spell their own name though as this is essential for when signing on, but beyond that they have no real academic training as they spent most of their school years bunking off.

The only certificate chavs collect is the ASBO (anti social behaviour order) and is treated as something to show off to mates.

Further Education

Once a chav leaves school then there is a halt on further learning, unless there is a government incentive that pays money for a chav to attend a college course. Of course, attend is all they do. They pay no attention to what's being taught and have no interest in the subject.

Chavs have little knowledge of the world around them and have little use for knowledge. They see it as evil and will only use knowledge if it gets them extra benefits or entry into someone else's car.

Employment

Generally none. Because of lack of education, the best chavs can get is the minimum wage. There's more economic sense to stay on the dole and claim jobseekers, housing and council tax benefit, and probably child benefit.

A chav boy walks into the jobcentre and says to the chap behind the desk "I'm looking for a job". The man says, "that's a coincidence, there's a job going here. It's a chauffeur job for a millionaire, you'll have to ferry his two daughters around. The downside is that you have to wear a uniform but the girls go on at least five holidays a year and you'll have to go with them to drive them. It's forty thousand a year salary". The chav replies "no, you're lying to me". The man replies, "well you started it".

Chav CV
                       Fings wot I did
                       Borstal
                       Dole
                       Community service
                       Prison
                       Dole

Entertainment

Because of lack of intelligence or eloquence, stuff like Shakespeare or Dickens would be like a foreign language. Chavs don't listen to music but anything with a heavy bass drum will do, if it rattles the rib cage then even better. They would listen to classical music if it has a deep bass drum mix in it.

Young chavs like to hang around brightly lit areas like shops and hurl abuse at the shoppers. Older chavs go to pubs or nightclubs, or anything with a thumping bass beat to it. Some chavs with money buy cars and just drive around to show everyone what fantastic (music?) they listen to (chavs don't care about the environment).

Chavs watch TV like anybody else but only stuff that's violent or requires little thought. Reality TV, foul-mouthed soaps and stealing cars type movies. They watch 'Police, Camera, Action' or 'Crimewatch' in the hope they will see themselves on the telly.

Dress

No dress sense at all.

The boys wear baggy trousers that hang down. They have to walk like Charlie Chaplin with bowed legs to stop their trousers from falling down. Useless when running from the police as they trip up the wearer but they think they are being cool showing off their underpants.

The girls' wear as little as possible or track suits. There has to be lots of piercings that must be shown at all times. Their hair is usually pulled back as tight as possible into a ponytail.

Both sexes must at absolutely all costs show they have a mobile phone and make their friends ring them up all the time, so that they can show people they are popular. And the phone must be more than just a phone; it must have all the latest gadgets on it.

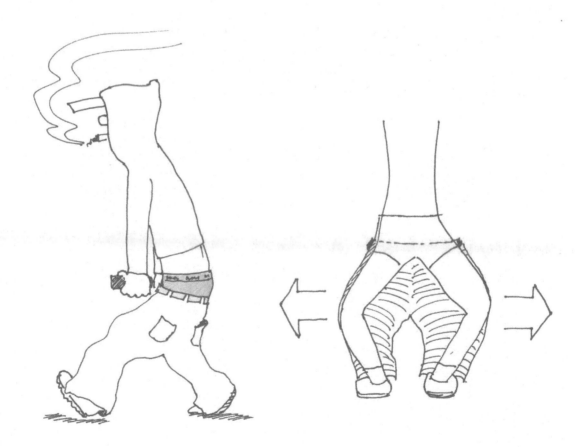

Young Chavs

Most young chavs have little respect for their parents, or vice versa. Whatever the situation, young chavs try not to stay at home and will go out to join their mates. The parents know where their children are but can't be bothered, as long the little perils are out of their hair.

As youngsters, they can only walk (or if they've nicked one) cycle, but only in large groups (pack mentality). However, some chavs obtain a motorcycle and will ride on the pavement or road with no helmet, lights, plates, tax or insurance with a large pack of chavs in tow.

It's widely viewed that young chavs are immune from the law and they know it. If they feel they want to pick on someone, they will. Do-gooders have ensured that youngsters remain unpunished irrespective of what they do.

Older Chavs

When chavs get older and get a job (ha ha) or their fortnightly dole cheque, they will spend their money on frivolous activities and stuff. Single boy chavs live at home with their parents and have no real out goings, and so spend their money on things like cars. And then…. they ruin their old bangers with useless add ons (high power sound systems and bolt ons).

Chav girls have children in order to obtain a council house, and then spend every opportune moment showing off their kids. Outside shops, in town, outside the pub, they will be there with their pushchairs and their little trophy.

Social Life

Chavs hang together in large numbers for safety and like to be apart from general society. They shun education, employment and general day-to-day activities like shopping or housework (that's what Mums are for).

Essential accessories are named clothing, mobile phone and cigarettes. Financial management is irrelevant to them as the moment they get money; it's spent on frivolous and useless items (alcohol and fags). If they haven't money for the pub or nightclub, then hanging outside a closed shop with their friends will do.

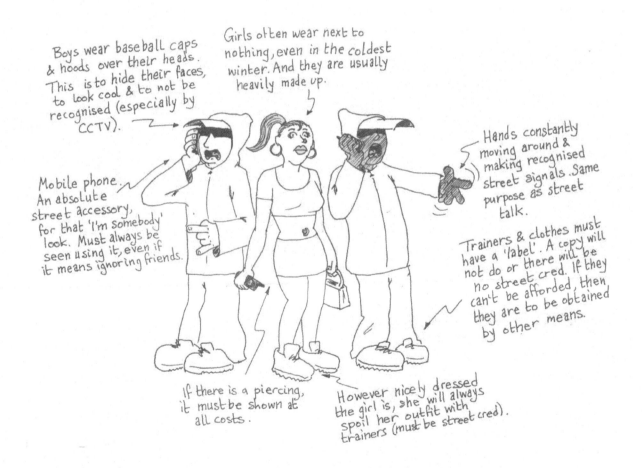

Holidays

In the last few years there has been an increase in low cost flights, chavs will often fly to exotic locations like Lanzarote or Torremolinos, Majorca or Ibiza, as long as they sell beer and have 24/7 nightclubs.

Sometimes a chav can get a free taxi service (has a useful add on known as a blue flashing light), but the destinations are limited. Under age chavs get to go home, while older chavs will spend a night at the Hotel d'Police. Has no star rating but does a complimentary breakfast. Sometimes, if a spell at the local cop shop leads to a court case then some chavs can get a free holiday as a reward for their acts of crime.

Street Talk no.1: performing good music

Street Talk no.2: being together with oneself

Street Talk no.3: being good at something

Chav Society

Chavs don't have real mates; they hang around other people in the street/area/pub etc. However, they do know several professional people: the local bobby, the judge, the community service and the jobseekers officer.

Chavs hang around with each other for safety; it's rare to see a chav on their own. When fighting, the old street rules of one on one don't apply, they just all pile in. Many people have been seriously hurt tangling with a chav. But often, a chav will start a fight for no reason at all and it doesn't matter who they pick on, as long the chav shows they rule.

Diet

Cheap, greasy and tasteless food especially from takeaways. They need to save their money for essentials like fags, booze and drugs. This is why chavs have greasy spotty faces because they aren't getting essential vitamins and minerals (do wot?). As the old saying goes, 'you are what you eat'.

Uses for Chavs

Not many, but like the old joke says, a chav is like a slinky because it has no real use but is fun to watch fall down the stairs.

Now that fox hunting has been banned, perhaps a fox substitute can be used by chavs.

Chavs in the evolutionary scale

It took about 5 million years for humans to evolve into the most intelligent animals on earth, but only a decade for a sub branch to regress into chavs. As long as chavs mate with other chavs, they will eventually reach a primordial soup (just like their brains are). With any luck, they will breed themselves out of existence.

Had Shakespeare been around today and had been a chav, he would have written Romeo & Juliet in chav language:

Juliet: Blut blut, Romeo La me bruv?
              You startin somethin
              You proper mingin man
              Geez uz yer phone

Romeo: Orr mate, wussup me homie?

Juliet: Yo bruv, you got dirt?
              You blatantly wicked man!
              We'd neva stop bein friends
              Safe innit like?
              Whatever
              You is one of da bad boyz
              You got a twenny pee man?
              My choons is well bangin man
              You is bubblin man
              I is well fit
              I need benefits bruv
              You dissing me? Do a nash

Chav Musicians

There is no such thing, although some musicians have chav leanings.

The only musical ability a chav would have is DJ'ing, the debate raging on for years as to whether a DJ is a musician or not. They don't actually play anything though, although there is supposed to be some skill in the mixing of pre-recorded records. If chavs do start a band, all they need is a drum machine and a microphone. All they need to do is press the 'GO' button and then talk over the beat, and then they have a 'song'.

Out of Town

The majority of chav environments tend to be cities and towns (close to cheap burger bars). However, occasionally chavs will escape to the peace and quiet of the countryside…and then ruin it. They make sure they bring with them their "banging choons (man)".

The environment is irrelevant to a chav as they have little understanding of ecology. They think a pork chop comes from the supermarket, and plants are planted whole (again from the supermarket). Climate change means nothing to them and is something they hear on the telly. Chavs will quite happily litter anywhere because they think it doesn't affect them, and that there is always someone to clear it up for them (remember, they don't pay council tax).

Chavs Effect on Society

They have no respect for anyone else and tend to do what they want, even if it means putting other peoples' lives in danger. They won't think twice about having a car race on the streets despite the fact that it's illegal. This is quite common on the streets of Britain, chavs will race their old bangers that have been souped up (without enhancing road holding etc) to a large crowd that gathers, usually informed on the internet that such an event is going to happen. It will continue all night long until the police come and break it up, or they seriously hurt someone.

Marriage

Normally a holy institution, however chavs see it as a means to get more benefits. Most of the time, a girl being single can have more money but sometimes there would be benefits to being married (the father won't have to pay maintenance).

Days Out

A day out to a chav would be expensive unless there is something worth seeing, like a car rally. Even if it's some obscure rally they will know about it, as it is useless information that cannot be used anywhere, except in a chav gathering where the chavs can show off their amazing knowledge of cars. The young chavs will spend hours drooling over an ordinary road car that has been done up with special bolt ons. The advertising stickers all over the car will add to the effect of a fast and exciting car.

Bravery

Something chavs know little about (otherwise they would join the army) as they rarely hang around on their own. In large groups they will feel safe enough to taunt people. They do this where they know people are going to be like shops and garages. They feel the world owes them a huge debt of respect (even thought they don't know the meaning of the word). If they see someone they that attracts their (limited) attention, they will pick on that person regardless. If the person chooses to walk away, they feel they've been insulted that they have been ignored. If the person replies back, they feel they've been insulted because of the wrong kind of respect. Either way, they will have their victim (and then claim that they have in fact been the victim of a disrespectful action).

Respect

The dictionary definition is "to show esteem, regard or consideration for". It is being aware of other people's feelings and taking steps to avoid confrontation.

However, chavs do not know the meaning of the word and bandy it about like some badge of recognition to other chavs. They want respect but the way they dress, speak and behave means that other people cannot show any respect towards a chav. Until chavs learn public etiquette, they will never gain respect in general society.

It's like the joke says: what's the first question you ask a chav at a quiz night? "What you looking at?"

Chavs to Outside Visitors

Should a chav be abducted by aliens, the outer world travellers may be mistaken they have abducted a representative of a primitive society. The chav, being the ambassador for the earth, may start interstellar war with his/her greeting of "what you looking at?"

Chav Rewards

If a chav wants the latest gadget or go on holiday, all they have to do is commit a crime. The more serious the crime, the greater the reward. This is due to the intervention of do-gooders claiming that chavs have had a poor growing up period that has affected their mental state, and they need care and love. What do-gooders don't realise is that chavs choose to be chavs, and besides, the do-gooders don't have to live next door to a chav as they can afford expensive houses and have little to do during the day except make up silly terms like 'height challenged' etc.

If by chance, a chav is sent to prison, then they will get their own room with a colour TV. Also they have the added benefit of extra-curricular education. There are courses like 'how to steal a car', 'how to fiddle the social security' and 'how to hack someone's computer for their personal details'.

The Single Chav

Most chavs spend time together and it is very rare to see a chav in their own. One way round this is to have to latest accessory known as a dog. Chavs don't like animals but will have the hardest meanest dogs to make them look cool, and they will give the dogs names that reflect the character they wish to portray like 'Tyson' or 'Soldier'.

When the chav needs to go to the pub or club, they will leave their dogs in the garden to bark all night. The residents will be powerless to stop the noise as the chav doesn't care (nor do the authourities). People have been on the brink of suicide trying to get the dog owner to look after their animal.

Chavs and the Law

They have no respect for the authourity of any kind. However, even though they cannot understand the legal gobbledegook, they know their legal rights inside out. They can commit crimes and know that they will be back on the streets again in no time at all.

Chav Foresight

They don't have any. Whereas most people can predict the outcome of certain events and take precautions to prevent danger, a chav's mind is empty. They cannot see the consequences of their actions and will cause untold misery on those who live around them. However, sometimes their mind will be filled with a thought such as the new 99p burger from McMeaties.

Not many people know this but male chavs have two brains, and they both reside between their legs, whereas most men will have a higher brain to (occasionally) override the lower ones.

Chavs with Money

They won't earn any significant amount of money through work, but if they are lucky enough to win the lottery then they will live a luxurious lifestyle for at least six months. Their money will run out quickly because they never learnt money management skills.

Again they will spend their money on frivolous and useless stuff, except it will be more expensive. They flash their money around effortlessly then wonder why it runs out eventually. It comes back to chav foresight.

Chavs on a Plane

Even Samuel L would have trouble with this lot. Chavs have no respect for authourity and will do what they like in flight even if it means putting other passenger's lives at risk. Even though the flight is two hours or less (Ibiza isn't far away), they still insist on behaving badly.

The snakes are probably easier to deal with, and less poisonous.

Chavs and Peace

Most people would like to see World Peace and live in harmony in their community with their neighbours. Not so the chav who likes nothing better than to see their community in ruins, especially if they can boast how they created it in that way. Public property is paid for by the public (which is why it is called public property) and is paid for by taxes. However, most chavs don't have a job so they don't have to pay for anything. They see public property as theirs to do with what they want (as said before they don't have the foresight to see what affect their actions have on society).

Horror Movies

Chav boys like nothing better than watching a scary horror movie and the more gore it has the better, nothing scares a chav except the prospect of getting a job

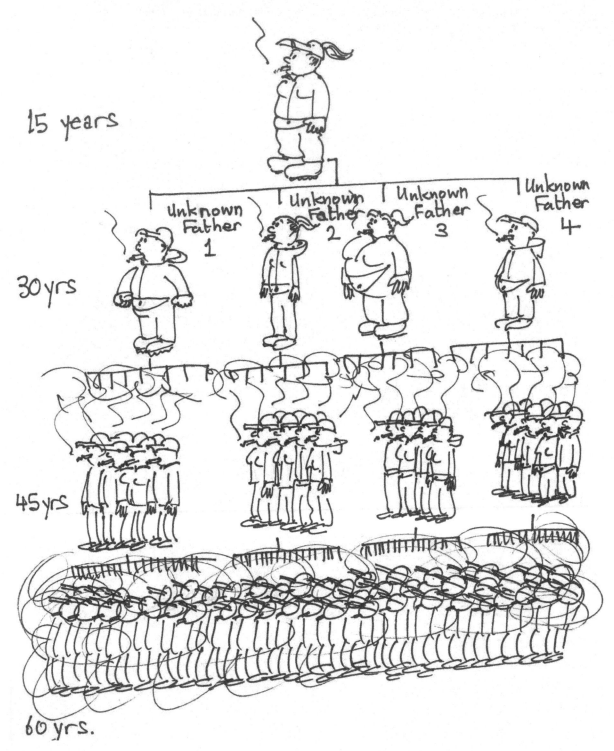

Chav Feelings

Mostly hate and anger, however they do love their kids (well they have enough of them) and express their love by blowing cigarette smoke in their faces. If the child complains they'll get the back of Mum or Dad's hand, however with the ban of corporal punishment the alternative is for the parents to swear loudly at their children not realising that even inside a house at high volumes the neighbours will hear what the children hear.

All the chavs in this book are not based on real characters and no chavs were harmed during the making of this book (unfortunately). To find out for yourself how lovable chavs are, check out the websites (available at the time of writing):

www.bebo.com/Profile

www.chavworld.co.uk/chav.htm

www.chavscum-resurrection.co.uk/forum/

www.chavscum-resurrection.co.uk

www.chavscum.co.uk

www.chavworld.co.uk